Original title:
The Stories We Live In

Copyright © 2025 Creative Arts Management OÜ
All rights reserved.

Author: Rosalie Bradford
ISBN HARDBACK: 978-1-80587-048-7
ISBN PAPERBACK: 978-1-80587-518-5

Flickers of Forgotten Light

In a world where socks go solo,
Dancing lost, like a drunken pogo.
Chasing dreams that sprout feet,
Then vanish in rapid retreat.

Pancakes flip with a hearty cheer,
While syrup plots its sweet frontier.
We laugh at the oddities faced,
With each silly mishap embraced.

A Tapestry of Voices

Whispers swirl in the kitchen air,
A potato narrates, so debonair.
Bananas plot to start a band,
Jamming groovy, all hand in hand.

Carrots and peas debate their fame,
While broccoli smiles, but feels no shame.
Every fruit and veggie takes a turn,
In a tale where laughter will always burn.

Contours of a Fleeting Moment

A cat in a hat struts with style,
While dogs just stare, confused for a while.
Jazz hands greet a wandering bee,
Who buzzes to tunes, full of glee!

Ticklish clouds float above us all,
While raindrops giggle at their own fall.
Moments flash by, a comic reel,
In this chaotic dance, what a feel!

Secrets Beneath the Surface

Underneath the floorboards lie,
A family of dust bunnies that sigh.
They gossip and snack on crumbs of bread,
Plotting adventures when no one's ahead.

The fridge hums softly, a secret keeper,
While pickles ponder, growing deeper.
In this realm of quirky delight,
Every snack has a tale, hidden from sight.

Serendipitous Encounters

In a café, spilled my tea,
A stranger laughed, right next to me.
We swapped tales of our clumsy falls,
And ended up with friends and brawls.

The bus delay was quite a treat,
Met a cat who stole my seat.
It purred and plotted world takeover,
While I just dreamed of my next endeavor.

Breathing Life into Old Pages

Found a book, forgot its name,
Dusty covers, not much fame.
But inside lurked some odd delight,
A talking fish—what a sight!

Each turn revealed a quirky twist,
Pineapple wars, you'd think we'd missed.
In laughter, we shook off the dust,
With every line, absurdity's thrust.

Colors of a Fading Memory

A purple hat, where did it go?
Last seen dancing at the show.
With neon lights and yellow shoes,
In our mishaps, we just can't lose.

We painted skies in shades of green,
Remember that raccoon with a sheen?
Colors fade, but laughter stays,
In painted lives, we found our ways.

The Mosaic of Our Lives

Fragments scattered on the floor,
Each piece hides a little more.
Jigsaw hearts and splintered dreams,
With every laugh, a broken seam.

In mismatched socks, we strut about,
Life's puzzle's wild, there's no doubt.
With silly hats and goofy dance,
We make our luck, we take our chance.

Vignettes of Vulnerability

In a coffee shop, I spilled my tea,
My pants now look like a leaky sea.
A stranger laughed, I gave a grin,
We shared a joke, a bond began.

My cat thinks she's a fierce queen,
But her battle cry's a soft whine, I've seen.
She stalks my feet with stealthy grace,
Then trips, and lands in her own space.

At family dinners, chaos reigns,
Chicken dances and silly games.
Uncle Joe wore socks with sandals on,
We all just laughed, 'til the night was gone.

Life's a stage with a script that's wild,
A dance of clowns, each heart a child.
In every blunder, a moment's gold,
Together we thrive, in laughter, we're bold.

A Journey Through Time's Lens

Remembering days of silly hats,
When we wore them while chasing cats?
Time ticked on, the world grew vast,
Yet here we are, with memories cast.

Old photos show us with freeze-frame grins,
Built castles from sand and paper bins.
We rode our bikes down the steepest hill,
Fell in the mud, but laughed with thrill.

Dial-up phones and matching socks,
Endless hours of playing with blocks.
Yet every dial was a dance with fate,
In the midst of laughter, we found our mates.

Now we share stories over a bite,
The past in our hearts, the future bright.
With every chuckle, time takes its toll,
But oh, those moments, they fill the soul.

Ways to Weave Connection

In a crowded room, we clash and collide,
With awkward laughs and nowhere to hide.
A wink was exchanged, a grin brought cheer,
And suddenly strangers felt very near.

Game nights lead to whole new schemes,
As we fight for glory and ice cream dreams.
The board may flip and laughter ensue,
In silly antics, friendships grew.

We text memes at the break of day,
A language of gifs to show we play.
Through quick replies and soft 'LOL',
Our hearts entwined, we're under its spell.

In shared adventures and random chats,
Unexpected bonds are where it's at.
Life's tapestry is woven bright,
With threads of joy that dance in light.

Footprints in the Sand of Time

On the beach, we wrote our names,
Only to laugh when the tide reclaimed.
The ocean giggled, 'I'll wash that away,'
As we skittered back, not wanting to stay.

Building castles, but they would fall,
With every wave, we'd heed the call.
Yet we danced like kings on shifting ground,
In sandy tales, our joy was found.

Time's a prankster, playing tricks,
One year we're here, and the next we mix.
But in each stumble and wild embrace,
We find our way, an endless chase.

In every grain, a story remains,
Of laughter echoing, and silly refrains.
So let's carve new paths, with giggles and stunts,
In this journey of life, we'll take our runs.

Heartbeats in the Fabric of Reality

In the quilt of moments, we patch and play,
A sock on the left, and shoes go astray.
With giggles and wiggles, we dance like a breeze,
Finding treasures in pockets, and crumbs in the keys.

Reality's fabric is stitched with a twist,
Our laughter it echoes, can't let it be missed.
Chasing the cats that we see in the sky,
We trip on the moss, and we never ask why.

Forgotten old sandwiches laugh in the sun,
While ants throw a party, they're just having fun.
With squirrels in tuxedos, they waltz in a line,
Who knew that a picnic could turn so divine?

As shadows grow long, we dance till we tire,
The dog wearing glasses thinks he's on fire.
In this patchwork of time, with whimsy we weave,
We find that the joy's only ours to believe.

Labyrinths of Yesterday's Heart

In yesterday's maze, we trip over tales,
With laughs that can echo, like wind in the sails.
A broken alarm clock sings songs of despair,
Yet still, we keep dancing without any care.

With crayons and scribbles, a map's drawn to fun,
Where tigers wear hats and pretend they can run.
A dandelion whispers secrets to the sun,
And wishes get tangled, oh, what have we done?

Through portraits of pets with eyes full of glee,
We paint all our problems with ice cream and tea.
Old melodies play as the clouds stretch and twirl,
While spacemen with sandwiches make heads all a swirl.

The clock ticks in rhythm, a hilarious beat,
As fortunes explode with each bump of the feet.
A world made of giggles, absurd and delight,
In labyrinths grand, we'll find laughter tonight.

Unscripted Adventures of the Mind

With socks on our hands, we march to the beat,
Imagining dragons that dance on their feet.
With coffee cups sailing on seas made of dreams,
We ride on the whim of our giggling themes.

The rules of the game say we must take a leap,
In puddles of marshmallows, we dive and we creep.
With thoughts like balloons that float high in the air,
We launch our imaginations, without any care.

A treetop talks softly, it shares all its lore,
About squirrels that write tales while eating their score.
We question the clouds, do they ever get sore?
As we tumble through laughter forever, encore!

So here's to the madness that shapes every day,
With giggles our compass, we wander and sway.
In adventures unscripted, we find our own charms,
With wonder and whimsy, let's feast on our swarms.

Fables Hidden in Common Places

In drawers full of socks, where stories abide,
A lone sock returns from a gnome's funny ride.
With muffins and magic, we stir up some fun,
As toasters tell tales of the bread that they've spun.

The garden sings loudly with whispers of ants,
While shadows are spinning in ridiculous pants.
With bees doing ballet on flowers with grace,
Who knew the sweet nectar held secrets to chase?

Underneath the old porch, we find a gold ring,
Held captive by crickets who dance and sing.
The garden gnomes gossip about who's out late,
In this ordinary world, the magic's first-rate!

So tiptoe through puddles, give each droplet a wink,
In stories so charming, we barely can think.
With humor our lantern, we light up the night,
Finding fables in places, where laughter takes flight.

The Echo of Generations Past

Grandpa tells tales with a twinkle,
Of dancing bears and a cat's sprinkles.
He swears that socks can fly, you see,
If we just believe in their legacy.

Auntie knits blankets with a frown,
Saying, "These patterns are from a clown!"
But every stitch holds a giggle tight,
As we all wonder who turned out the light.

Uncle's got secrets in a jar of jam,
He claims it holds the truth of who I am.
But try as I might, it just tastes sweet,
With a hint of mystery and a wigged-out beet.

Through laughter and tales, we dance in glee,
Connecting the dots in our family tree.
For in every chuckle, both loud and slight,
Lives a timeless truth, hidden in plain sight.

Stanzas of Fleeting Moments

Tick-tock, the clock has a mind of its own,
It trips over minutes, and then it's all gone.
My cereal thinks it's a swimming pool,
As I dive in with a spoon, feeling quite cool.

A dog chased its tail, in a dizzying race,
Only to stumble and fall flat on his face.
Mom yelled, 'It's dinner!' but where has the time fled?
My sandwich is waiting, but I'm lost in my head.

Kids on bicycles zip past with their cheers,
Waving at clouds as they conquer their fears.
With laughter like music floating through air,
We savor the moments we truly can share.

So let's seize these seconds before they escape,
And jot down our fun in a silly scrapbook shape.
For laughter is gold, and time is quite funny,
In the stanzas of life, we find rich honey.

Reflections in a Cloudy Sky

Clouds gather like gossip under bright sun's gaze,
They whisper of rain in a laugh-inducing haze.
A rainbow pops up with a wink and a shove,
Telling me that even storms can be love.

A pigeon struts proudly, a king in his realm,
Claiming the park bench as his royal helm.
He coos to the clouds, asking where they've been,
While ducks practice yoga, splashing in din.

The trees sway and giggle with every soft breeze,
While squirrels pretend they're expert trapeze.
Together they flourish in sky's silly grace,
Creating a circus, a whimsical place.

So let's laugh at the clouds and dance in the rain,
For life has its puddles, and joy is our gain.
With each droplet falling, let's cheer and let fly,
The giggles and chuckles that dance in the sky.

A Symphony of Silent Stories

In a library corner, the books start to chatter,
As characters giggle, 'Oh, what's the matter?'
Pages flip over with secrets to tell,
Whispering loudly as they weave their spell.

An old globe spins, in a dizzy delight,
It thinks it knows everything, morning to night.
"I've seen all the places, a wild world tour!"
It brags, but we know it's just trying to score.

The clock on the wall clicks with a jest,
"Oh, please don't ask me, I'm just doing my best!"
While chairs creak a tune, dancing side to side,
A symphony plays in this cozy reside.

So let's gather our tales, let laughter abound,
In silent stories where joy can be found.
For life's quite a melody, playful and spry,
Each moment a note in the grandest goodbye.

Mythos of the Mundane

In socks unmatched, I boldly stride,
My coffee cup's a trusted guide.
The toaster hums a daily tune,
While laundry shrieks, 'I need a boon!'

The cat, a sage, on windowsill,
Catches sunbeams, plotting still.
The fridge's light, a beacon bright,
Beholds my snack, a pure delight.

With errands stacked like ancient tomes,
I navigate through dust and gloams.
Each trip to town, an epic quest,
For snacks, and naps, my heart's request.

At night I ponder what I've done,
Did I feed the cat? Was it fun?
In chaos danced, my weird charade,
Are these the tales my life has made?

Navigator of Ephemeral Moments

A sneeze on cue, my grand debut,
The world spins round, I slip on dew.
In crowded rooms, I tell a jest,
As laughter winks, my favorite fest.

Sidewalks pulse with mighty throngs,
Each stroll feels like I could belong.
The pigeons gossip, strut their stuff,
While I just laugh—enough is tough!

In waiting lines for sushi rolls,
I ponder deeply life's goals.
That fortune cookie whispers sweet,
But I just crave more spiced meats.

As clocks tick softly into night,
I count my quirks, a pure delight.
In fleeting joy, I find my song,
In moments brief, we all belong.

Voices of the Unwritten

With pens in hand, we scribble dreams,
On napkins stained with coffee beams.
The stories wait, unbound, untold,
In coffee shops, we're brave and bold.

A whispered joke shared with a friend,
Turns into laughs that never end.
In quirky tales of cats and dogs,
We find our truth in friendly fogs.

The sidewalk cracks hold secrets tight,
While stars above twinkle their light.
Each fleeting laugh a bond we weave,
In every moment, we believe.

The world's a page, all fresh and new,
With every glance, another view.
Here's to the quirks, the tales unsung,
In laughter's arms, our hearts are young.

Scattered Pages of Our Existence

I trip on thoughts like scattered leaves,
As wisdom hides, the heart deceives.
Unruly pens and coffee stains,
Mark all the highs and silly pains.

In line at stores, we share a blush,
The checkout beep, a comical hush.
The clerk's a poet, in his flair,
As he recites my total with care.

With random chats and silly sighs,
We cultivate our shared goodbyes.
Each bump along this bumpy ride,
Crafts laughter strong we cannot hide.

So here we dwell on life's abstract,
In silly scenes, we find our pact.
With pages torn, yet stories flow,
These scattered bits keep spirits aglow.

Whispers Beneath Our Skin

In the café, tales take flight,
A cat in a hat steals the light.
Cupcakes dance on the edge of the plate,
While squirrels complain about their fate.

Grandma's secret recipe's a laugh,
Her chicken soup's always a gaffe.
A pinch of this with a dash of that,
Turns a feast into a combat spat!

Echoes of Unsaid Words

In the park, a dog wears a tie,
As pigeons giggle and squirrels fly.
Mismatched socks tell tales of woe,
While the ice cream melts in a glorious show.

With whispers lost in the breeze,
A frog croaks jokes with such ease.
The moon rolls its eyes at our plight,
As shadows dance in the soft twilight.

The Fabric of Our Journeys

Tangled yarn on a sunny day,
Knitted hats that refuse to stay.
A scarf so long it trips the cat,
While grandma shouts, 'Don't you dare sit flat!'

Each thread spins tales of laughter and cheer,
Of awkward hugs and a missing deer.
Our journeys woven with stitches profound,
In a patchwork world, we're glory-bound!

Lives Unfolding in Chapters

Every morning, a new page to write,
A sock in the toaster? Oh, what a sight!
Bedhead dreams of a world so bright,
Where ducks in sunglasses take flight.

The neighbor's cat reads poetry aloud,
As children giggle, forming a crowd.
Each chapter is a giggle, a jest,
In the book of lives, it's all of the best!

Wrinkles of Time

The clock just ticked, but who's counting?
Life's a stage, with laughter mounting.
A slip on a banana, oh what a sight,
We dance through the chaos, morning till night.

Grandma's tales make her eyes sparkle,
While dad tells jokes that make us cackle.
Spilling coffee, wearing mismatched shoes,
These little mishaps are our daily news.

A distant past where we once tumbled,
Finding great joy when life leaves us humbled.
A wrinkle here, a wrinkle there,
Laugh lines etched in every care.

With every giggle, we patch the seams,
Life's a sitcom filled with funny memes.
So raise a toast, let the fun unwind,
In this wild ride, what joy we find!

The Quiet Chronicles

In whispers soft, the tales begin,
Of unmatched socks, oh where've they been?
A silent scream when the cat steals food,
Life's quirks played out, never subdued.

In corners where dust bunnies reside,
Lie secrets of naps and dreams that collide.
Under the radar, amidst the hush,
We find our giggles in the quiet rush.

The neighbor's dog wears a silly hat,
While kids play checkers with a friendly cat.
Sipping tea while gossip runs wild,
The quiet moments, we've all been styled.

So listen close to the tales untold,
In chuckles shared, pure joy unfolds.
With a wink, we keep our secrets tight,
In the melody of whispers, we delight.

Untold Truths in a Loud World

In a world so loud, we find our fun,
Silly old hats for everyone!
Balancing groceries, talking too fast,
A circus of life, we've all cast.

The toaster pops, the dog won't behave,
Each little chaos, our lives we save.
The truth is out, in muffled tones,
When laughter echoes in every home.

A missing shoe, the coffee's too strong,
We navigate life like a karaoke song.
The sirens wail, the kids break free,
What truth emerges when we just let be?

So in this ruckus, take your stance,
Embrace the chaos, give life a chance.
In laughter's embrace, we find our peace,
Where happiness blooms, our joys increase.

Threads of Connection

In tangled yarns, our stories weave,
With giggles shared, we all believe.
A connection made with a wink or grin,
In this playful game, we always win.

A neighbor's laugh, a stranger's dance,
Life's little moments are our chance.
Fumbling words, a missed high-five,
These threads of life keep us alive.

Silly dances in the grocery lane,
Chasing our pets in the summer rain.
With every stumble and fortuitous fumble,
We build a tapestry that never tumbles.

So gather 'round for the playful tale,
Where laughter's wind fills every sail.
In this grand weave, our hearts align,
With threads of connection, our joys entwine.

Ripple Effects of Kindness

A smile can travel far and wide,
Like a pebble tossed on a lake's tide.
You laugh, I laugh, and the world spins bright,
Turning grumpy frowns into pure delight.

With cookies shared and jokes exchanged,
We rearrange the dull and unchanged.
Your silly dance, a joyful spark,
Sends ripples out, igniting the dark.

Labyrinth of the Unexpected

Life's a maze of twist and bends,
Where ducks in tuxedos meet chicken friends.
You think you're lost, but wait, surprise!
A disco ball lights up the skies.

Around each corner, laughter's found,
With wobbling hedgehogs that spin around.
Even the walls may crack a joke,
Just when you think you've gone up in smoke!

Shadows and Silhouettes

In the twilight, shadows dance and sway,
A lanky figure goes the wrong way.
Is that a ghost? Oh wait, it's you!
Trying to moonwalk in a shoe.

Silhouettes laugh in the fading light,
A snickering cat and a dog in flight.
With mismatched socks and hats so bold,
Together we weave stories yet untold.

Our Collective Memoir

With crayons scribbled on pages bright,
We sketch our lives in pure delight.
An odd tale here, a weird chapter there,
Like accidentally dyeing your mother's hair.

Each mishap recorded, a giggle in style,
Turning chaos to laughter, mile after mile.
When we gather 'round to share our day,
Every folly makes the heart sway.

The Canvas of Our Adventures

We painted skies with mismatched hues,
Splashing laughter, dodging blues.
With every spill and vibrant stroke,
We crafted tales, giggles bespoke.

The sun was bright, our hats were askew,
Chasing ice cream trucks, a thrilling view.
We danced like fools in a summer rain,
Collecting moments, joy was our gain.

A treasure map on a paper plate,
Finding wonders that we create.
Each winding path, a funny plot,
In our whimsical world, we loved a lot.

With shoes untied, we raced the breeze,
Giggling at ants and climbing trees.
The canvas wide, our hearts so free,
In every misstep, we found glee!

Unfolding the Heart's Narrative

In the book of us, there's quite a twist,
With each page turned, and a grin on our list.
We pen our dreams with silly ink,
And share our thoughts over food and drink.

Once I wrote 'adventure' and made a mess,
Found a frog in the pocket of my dress.
Your laugh was loud, my cheeks turned red,
In the chapters of laughter, all worries fled.

We scribble secrets in crumpled notes,
And race the clock on silly boats.
With every quirk, our tales unfold,
In the warmth of friendship, we find gold.

The stories linger like the scent of pie,
As we plot and plan and let joy fly.
With every mishap and giggle shared,
Our unfolding tale is perfectly bared.

Reflections in a Distant Mirror

In a mirror far, what do we see?
A pair of clowns sipping jasmine tea.
With goofy grins and one misplaced shoe,
Our laughter echoes, it's all so true.

We practice winks and silly faces,
In a world of mirrors and funny places.
Each reflection shows a different story,
Of dance moves gone wrong, and shared glory.

Oh, the mishaps that time has spun,
Like trying to cook while you run.
With a toast to ourselves, we often cheer,
For the clowns we are, the moments dear.

So here's to mirrors, the frolicsome view,
To the heart's reflection, and me and you.
In every giggle and wild surprise,
The truth of our mirth forever flies.

Portraits of Shared Tomorrows

In future frames, we paint with zest,
With goofy hats, we're quite the best.
Our shared tomorrow brims with cheer,
In each little dream, we hold so dear.

With every portrait, a silly pose,
Caught mid-laugh, with mismatched clothes.
We sketch our plans with a whimsical quirk,
In the gallery of life, we joyfully lurk.

Together we stumble through ups and downs,
Creating a blend of smiles and frowns.
Every mischief holds a tiny grace,
In the canvas of chaos, we find our place.

So let's fast-forward to the days ahead,
With silly antics, our lives well-fed.
Each portrait a giggle, a dance, a song,
In the shared tomorrows, where we belong!

Map of Silent Hopes

In a land where socks go to hide,
There's a map of dreams, a silly tide.
With each lost shoe, a tale sat tight,
Chasing rainbows, dodging daylight.

We scribble lines on napkins fair,
Eating lunch while unaware.
A jellybean emperor, crowned with glee,
Reigns over crumbs of a grand spree.

With bookmarks stained from juice spills,
Heroic tales of fridge raids thrill.
Each yogurt cup, a saga spun,
Who knew that spoons could make it fun?

Exploring worlds, we laugh and grin,
For every fail, there's always win.
So here's to maps, though they may fade,
In every twist, hilarity's laid.

Narratives Yet to be Written

On a page where doodles dance and sing,
A penguin dreams of being a king.
With a tiny crown and fanciful wings,
He rules the land of sock-puppet things.

A cat in glasses reads the news,
While sipping tea from colorful shoes.
Each headline makes the kittens roar,
As they plan their very own galore.

With jellyfish swimming in the sky,
Banana boats set sail nearby.
As dolphins play hopscotch on land,
These tales are silly, quirky, and grand.

So grab your pens, it's time to create,
These narratives shall not wait!
In laughter loud, our stories bloom,
With every chuckle, we light the room.

Footprints on the Pages

A cookie trail leads to the fridge,
Where crumbs whisper tales from a bridge.
Each nibble taken, a story shared,
Of midnight raids when no one cared.

Gnome-shaped footprints on the floor,
From garden quests to the junk drawer.
A skateboard dream with a wobbly twist,
Every adventure, too fun to miss.

The cat's been writing on my desk,
Her literature? A furry mess.
She claims each paw print is profound,
Yet all we see is fluff abound.

Through crooked lines and silly rhymes,
We find the joy in silly times.
For every laugh, a story we trade,
In this wild world, we're never afraid!

Fables of Forgotten Days

In a cupboard where the dishes rattle,
Lie fables of a dinner battle.
The green peas staged a grand revolt,
Against broccoli, their villainous bolt.

A sleeping cat, a knight's domain,
Guarding treasure, yet claims no fame.
Each yarn spun of whisker-wisdom,
A feline saga, pure rhythm.

While socks conspire from the laundry heap,
They form a league, a promise to keep.
With plans for mischief, a wild spree,
To snatch the remote and laugh with glee.

In tales long lost, we find our tune,
With giggles rising like a balloon.
So here's to fables, both odd and bright,
In every twist, we find delight.

Portraits Beneath the Stars

Underneath those twinkling lights,
I swear I'm an astronaut in tights.
Zooming past in my cardboard car,
Finding pizza places near and far.

The moon winks at me with a grin,
Saying, "Hey buddy, where've you been?"
Stories told by crickets' chirps,
As I dance like a fool, tripping over jerks.

Tonight's the night I'll wear my crown,
King of the backyard, never feeling down.
With my trusty sidekick, a squirrel named Bill,
We plot hilarious heists with a giggle and thrill.

So here we are, just dreaming wide,
On a space trip down the slip 'n slide.
With laughter echoing in the night air,
Painting portraits of nonsense everywhere.

Journeys Through Time's Tapestry

In my living room, a wormhole spins,
Offering journeys and colorful whims.
Riding a cat through a breeze so light,
We chase down the doughnuts lost to flight.

I met a wizard with a magic mop,
Who taught me how to taco-flop.
He said, "Time is a stretchy, funny thing,
Join me in chaos; hear the laughter we bring!"

Before I knew, I was in the past,
Eating shrimps in a pirate's cast.
"Yarrr!" said the captain, wearing a hat,
While I juggled fish and said — "Look at that!"

The future called; said it missed me too,
With robot friends and a kangaroo.
Adventuring through layers, spinning around,
With giggles and mayhem, that's where I'm found.

Reflections from the Quiet Corners

In the alcove, whispers rise and fall,
Of sock puppets having a ball.
Gathering secrets with a grin,
As the couch cushions hold their chin.

The cat judges with a regal stance,
While I trip over shoes in a clumsy dance.
Mirror, mirror, can you see?
The chaos that seems to follow me?

A ghost in the corner, laughing loud,
As I play the jester, head unbowed.
Toilet paper rolls become my stage,
With epic tales of cats, chaos, and rage.

So join the parade, it's quite a show,
In quiet corners, where silliness grows.
Reflections murmur of laughter and light,
In a room that dreams through the night.

Lives Interlaced in Shadowed Light

In the corner where shadows play,
Lurks a raccoon who steals the day.
He sprinkles mischief like fairy dust,
With tales of treasure hidden in rust.

Oh, the fables told with a twist of fate,
Of socks lost and a goat acting great.
We laugh at the tales as they weave and curl,
In the soft glow of night, let imaginations whirl.

Each shadow holds a secret dance,
While I tumble and prance, taking my chance.
Star-shaped cookies and stories collide,
As we play hide and seek in the stars that we ride.

In this tapestry of laughter and light,
Where whimsy reigns and dreams take flight,
Our lives are painted in shades of delight,
Interlaced forever in shadowed light.

Diaries of the Heart

In my diary, I wrote a tale,
Of a cat who thought he could sail.
He jumped on a boat, so proud and spry,
But forgot that he couldn't fly.

Each page turned, more quirks unfold,
Like my goldfish who fancies bold.
He swims in circles, dreaming of fame,
While the snail next door rolls his eyes in shame.

There's a section on my morning toast,
Where butter plots to be a ghost.
It slides right off, causing a mess,
And leaves crumbs that I must confess.

So laugh with me, in this quirky ride,
For every heart holds laughter inside.
Our lives are tales of silly delight,
With every giggle shining bright.

Threads of Our Existence

We weave our lives with threads of cheer,
Like my sock that vanished in the gear.
One's a loner, the other a pair,
They whisper secrets in the air.

In the tapestry of every day,
A sandwich spills its mayonnaise play.
Each splat a burst of joy and wit,
Creating chaos in my lunch kit.

I once met a shoe that wished to dance,
But tripped on laces, oh what a chance!
With every step, a stumble and twirl,
Life's rhythm is a funny whirl.

So stitch your quirks into delight,
For every thread makes the fabric bright.
In our jumbled, cluttered existence,
Lies the humor in every instance.

Portraits of Our Encounters

I paint a picture of my last date,
With spaghetti tangled on my plate.
He laughed so hard, sprayed sauce like a squirt,
His shirt a canvas, oh what a flirt!

The artist next door drew a space cat,
Who claimed it could chat, imagine that!
With a flick of its tail and a wink of its eye,
It ordered a pizza, oh my, oh my!

My friend had a dream of flying a kite,
But it tangled in trees, oh what a sight!
While the squirrels cheered, launching a plan,
To commandeer it, those crafty clan!

In these portraits, laughter does blend,
Each snapshot of fun, a perfect send.
Our encounters, a canvas bold,
With strokes of joy, forever told.

In the Margins of Memory

In my margins, notes like little birds,
Dancing around, and singing words.
They chirp of coffee spills and silly falls,
Of awkward waves and misheard calls.

A doodle features my pet goldfish,
Who dreams of being a cat—oh, what a wish!
He practices pouncing from his glass,
But flops instead, like a clumsy lass.

Each corner holds a memory bright,
Like my mom's hat that took flight one night.
It flew on a breeze, a wobbly soar,
And landed on a neighbor's door.

So flip through these margins, feel the glee,
In every scribble, there's a spree.
For laughter lingers in every line,
In our quirky sense of time divine.

Sketches of Distant Places

On a map of dreams, we draw our lines,
Cacti wear hats, sipping on brines.
Sailing on rainbows, we'll soon find,
A giraffe runs a café, quite one of a kind.

Chasing the clouds, we dance on air,
A fox in a suit, kindly stops to stare.
In pockets of time, we throw our care,
Finding lost socks—oh, what a rare fare!

With penguins that paint and monkeys that sing,
Each twist and turn is a curious fling.
The sun wears sunglasses, a humorous thing,
While wind whispers secrets that laughter will bring.

So pack up your dreams, let's roam wild and free,
On this grand adventure, just you and me.
With silly mishaps, oh can't you see?
Life's humorous paths stretch endlessly!

The Tapestry of Us

In colors so bright, we weave our thread,
A cat plays chess—what a life, we said!
With hiccups and giggles, our laughter is spread,
Each moment a patchwork, adventure ahead.

Knitting with noodles, we stir up delight,
A dragon with sunglasses takes off in flight.
Building a fortress with pillows at night,
Imagining monsters that give hugs, how bright!

With mismatched socks and shoes laced with fun,
A race with potatoes—oh, who's going to run?
We're a circus of oddballs, each joke weighed and done,
In this colorful saga, we shine like the sun.

So join in this dance on this quirky old floor,
With friends by our side, there's always more.
In this wacky old house, we forever explore,
Writing our moments, together in lore!

Unraveled Truths

In a world of wonders, we twist and twirl,
With umbrellas for hats, laughter's our pearl.
An octopus juggles, oh what a whirl,
While squirrels conduct, in a grand little whirl.

Our shoes have long stories, mischief and grime,
A taco is dancing, celebrating sublime.
In the oddest of quests, we journey through time,
With each funny mishap, we discover the rhyme.

With tales told by socks and cheese as our muse,
A marmot in pajamas, who'll gladly refuse.
Life's quirks are the canvas; we hastily choose,
To color the bland, turning chaos to blues.

So scribble your dreams in a notebook of jest,
With giggles and giggles, say who needs a rest?
In these silly truths, we're all truly blessed,
In this fun little world, we laugh with the best!

Letters Never Sent

I wrote you a letter, but lost it in space,
It landed on Mars, much to my disgrace.
With aliens giggling, they borrowed my lace,
Their dance moves are bold, quite a wild chase.

I scribbled a postcard from clouds up above,
With rainbows and giggles, I sent you my love.
But it fell in a puddle—oh what a shove!
Now frogs wear my notes, croaking dreams like a dove.

With crayons and markers, my words turned to art,
A masterpiece drifting, torn pieces apart.
But each little scribble, a laugh from the heart,
In letters unwritten, you played a fine part.

So here's to the messages, we never relayed,
With funky old stories, our life's masquerade.
In this world of wonders, the fun never fades,
In letters unsealed, our laughter cascades!

Journey Through the Heart's Maze

Lost in the twists of my own mind,
Every corner has a laugh to find.
A squirrel steals my sandwich, oh what a feat,
A maze of giggles, it can't be beat.

I bump into walls made of candy canes,
They taste so sweet, cure all my pains.
A cat in a hat gives me a wink,
"You lost?" he says, "Just follow the pink!"

Steps lead to puddles filled with lime,
I leap and splash in chaotic rhyme.
Each bounce takes me deeper in play,
In this heart's maze, I'll happily stay.

With every twist, more laughter grows,
Unraveling tales only my heart knows.
In this wacky world, I'll twirl and sway,
Forever lost, but hey, that's okay!

Curated Moments of Joy

In the fridge lies a cake that's far too big,
Each slice a moment, a sweet little jig.
I serve it with sprinkles, a dash of glee,
Creating memories, just wait and see.

A trampoline party with friends in tow,
Each bounce a giggle, the fun starts to grow.
A fall turns to laughter, as we take a dive,
In curated chaos, we feel so alive.

Cracking jokes like cracking eggs,
With laughter that dances on all our legs.
These moments, a feast, so tasty and bright,
In our joyful gathering, everything feels right.

Snuggling under blankets, stories unfold,
Some spoken whispers, some legends retold.
Curated with love, every tale a spree,
In this glorious gallery, come jump with me!

Dances in the Rain

Raindrops tap-dance on my window sill,
Each plop and splash makes my heart thrill.
I toss aside worries, forget my frown,
Join the parade, let's twirl in town.

Puddles become stages for each joyful leap,
While icicles giggle, secrets they keep.
I spin like a ballerina, soaking it through,
This wet little world, only for two.

Umbrellas flipped upside, rainbow parade,
Our dance in the rain—oh, how it's played!
With each silly slip, laughter reigns free,
In a whimsical waltz, just you and me.

Each raindrop a laugh, each splash our song,
In nature's embrace, we can't go wrong.
So let's twirl together, through puddles we'll slide,
In this dance of the rain, joy takes us for a ride!

The Weight of Shared Secrets

Whispers like bubbles float through the air,
Each fragile secret, without a care.
We giggle and grumble, under the sun,
Those silly confessions, oh what fun!

An old lady's hat, a dog that sings,
The weight of our secrets is lighter than things.
With each little chuckle, the world feels right,
As we share our tales, hearts glow so bright.

A slip of the tongue, a mischievous prank,
We trade our oddities like notes in a bank.
In a vault of laughter, we lock them all tight,
The weight of our whispers spreads joy in flight.

So let's hold these secrets like treasure, indeed,
While we dance through the day, planting joy's seed.
In the garden of giggles, let's grow and bloom,
The weight of our hearts will fill any room!

Insights from the In-between

In a world of mismatched socks,
We trip over life's silly blocks.
Coffee spills and laughter erupts,
Misadventures, oh how we're cupped.

Friends debate which snack's the best,
Is it cheese puffs, or maybe zest?
In the chaos, truth finds a way,
To giggle at our clumsy play.

We juggle dreams of grand design,
With stories that are yours and mine.
Each twist brings a curious laugh,
Like dance moves gone wrong at half.

So let's toast to the slips and trips,
And savor life through wobbly sips.
For in this dance of fate and chance,
We find the joy in our mishap dance.

Reflections from the Edge of Tomorrow

Peering into tomorrow's lens,
We giggle at our make-believe trends.
With robots serving pancakes tall,
Life's future isn't dreary at all.

We chase after our flying dreams,
Through foam party plots and silly schemes.
Each day's a meme, a playful tease,
Where laughter floats like autumn leaves.

Zooming cars and talking cats,
We throw our hands up—where's the facts?
Yet revel in our wacky fate,
And dance with joy like it's all great.

The clock ticks odd, the world's a show,
With punchlines hidden in the flow.
For tomorrow's edge can surely bend,
To funny tales that never end.

Journeys of the Wanderer

A wanderer trips down rugged roads,
Finding treasures in silly toads.
With mismatched luggage and wild hair,
He's the king of unexpected flair.

Maps with scribbles, no clear route,
He dances, laughs, and gives a shout.
Each pit stop's filled with tales so grand,
Of ice cream mountains and jellybeans land.

At the beach, he builds a sandcast tower,
Only to find it swamped by a shower.
Yet through the rain, he starts to sing,
Finding joy in everything.

So here's to the ones who roam so free,
With goofy grins, and hearts with glee.
For every journey adds a twist,
In whimsical tales that can't be missed.

Serene Echoes of the Past

In quiet corners of memory's hall,
We hear the echoes of laughter's call.
Where mischief brewed and dreams took flight,
And silly dances lasted all night.

Old photos show our awkward phase,
With wild hair and those shocking ways.
Each snapshot, a story of smiles and charms,
In a time when we fit in our moms' arms.

Bicycles raced on streets of gold,
Tales of friendships forever told.
With ice cream fights and hide-and-seek,
The past was a labyrinth, joyous and meek.

So let us cherish those moments rare,
For in the gentle whispers of air,
Lie nuggets of wisdom, fun and bright,
In echoes of joy, our hearts take flight.

Unwritten Songs of the Night

In shadows deep, where laughter plays,
A cat performs in curious ways.
The moon takes notes, a silent bard,
As squirrels moonwalk, fairly bizarre.

With stars that twinkle, a disco ball,
Each critter dances, both short and tall.
They gossip softly, in secret tones,
Of midnight snacks and mischief's moans.

An owl rolls eyes at the lively crew,
While raccoons raid bins, 'Oh, what a view!'
They sing of dreams, both weird and bright,
In this jolly world of the playful night.

Dreams Lost in Time

Once I had a dream, so grand,
That involved a dancing giant band.
But I woke up to find it all,
Replaced by socks, a laundry sprawl.

In a world where tea was meant for kings,
And squirrels wore hats, potentially with blings.
But reality checked, like a friend too bold,
Kicking me back, with stories told.

The clock keeps ticking, with playful jests,
As I chase after what I want next.
But finding my keys? That's the real climb,
In this labyrinth of misplaced time.

Whims of the Wandering Mind

Oh, the brain, a circus full of cheer,
A juggler of thoughts that take a queer steer.
Should I wear pants, or just stay in bed?
Why do I ponder what cats have said?

Turning ideas like an old school wheel,
Riding the waves of an endless reel.
Searching for snacks in a fridge so bare,
While crafting sonnets that go nowhere.

I bid adieu to a thought that's shy,
Who knew it had wings? It's off to fly!
With whispers of nonsense, I chase and pine,
In this maze of whims, I'm feeling divine.

Seasons of Unlikely Friendship

Winter brought snowflakes and a knit hat,
And I shared my lunch with a friendly cat.
We sat by the fire, just sharing our dreams,
Me of warm beaches, and it of hot creams.

Spring came a-dancing with polka-dot bloom,
I found a lost shoe that was taking up room.
A duck waddled by with a curious honk,
They said 'Befriend me!' and I said, 'Let's clonk!'

Summer sizzled with carefree delight,
We planned a barbecue under the night.
The raccoons gatecrashed, not on the list,
But how can you hate when the sun's in bliss?

Fall whispered secrets in colors of gold,
As friendships bloomed, a sight to behold.
From critters to friends, this patchwork we weave,
In seasons of laughter, we joyously cleave.

Whispers of Untold Paths

In a world where socks play hide-and-seek,
The cat plans a heist with a piece of meat.
Butterflies wear glasses, looking quite chic,
While ants throw a party, dancing on their feet.

A fridge hums a tune, soft as a breeze,
While dishes conspire, whispering with ease.
The spoon is a knight, the fork a tease,
In a realm of kitchen fables, laughter will please.

Puddles reflect dreams of daring, bold quests,
The postman is a wizard delivering jest.
Each day a new chapter, a riddle to test,
A tale told by giggles, we're simply the best.

So gather your stories, don't hide them away,
In laughter we'll find a bright, silly way.
From crayon-scribbled vows to games we play,
Life's a wild circus—a comical foray.

Echoes in Forgotten Pages

Dusty tomes whisper secrets untold,
A dragon discussed in a line that is bold.
With wizards and witches, all painted in gold,
Beneath a cat's paw, their stories unfold.

Tea cups hold battles, where marshmallows fight,
The spoon spins around, a dizzying sight.
Every page turned, is a giggle-filled night,
As gnomes lead the charge, to laughter's delight.

In libraries, cats dance, a quirky parade,
Bookmarks are pirates, a whimsical trade.
Forgotten adventures, in paper they wade,
Where silly invaders sneak in unafraid.

So cherish these echoes, these giggles and grins,
In the tales of our past, the laughter begins.
Turn up the volume, let the fun spin,
For every lost story brings joy that wins.

Tales Woven in Dreams

In dreams' playful realm, noodle monsters roam,
With jellybean crowns, they make their home.
In the land of pajamas, the giggles foam,
Where pillows are castles, we're never alone.

A rubber duck captain sails seas of shampoo,
While clouds play violins, serenading the dew.
In this wacky adventure, a quest that is true,
We jump on the moon, with a hop and a chew.

A mouse with a mustache recites silly prose,
Lemonade fountains where laughter just grows.
Every snicker and hiccup is simply how it goes,
In these dreamy escapades, anything shows.

So sleep with a grin, let the whimsy ignite,
For in every dream, the funny takes flight.
Each moment a giggle, a sparkling delight,
In the fabric of dreams, life's humor shines bright.

Chronicles of Everyday Heroes

Supermarket knights with carts full of snacks,
Battle the boredom with laughter that cracks.
Through piles of laundry, they follow the tracks,
In search of lost socks and heroic hijinks that max.

Bus drivers are wizards, steering spells on the street,
Transforming calm mornings to rhythmic heartbeats.
With smiles as weapons, they scatter the heat,
Turning waits into dances—a joyous retreat.

Baristas serve coffee with a sprinkle of cheer,
Their espresso machines whirling, no need for fear.
In every cup, magic is brewed, oh dear,
With laughter as foam, the world's woes disappear.

So raise a toast to heroes, both near and within,
Whose laughter ignites the adventure we spin.
In the chronicles of joy, let the fun begin,
Life's a grand saga, it's a riot to win!

Vignettes of Hope and Grit

In a town where socks come loose,
A cat plays chess with a moose.
Each move they make is quite absurd,
While the townsfolk laugh, their vision blurred.

A baker dreams of flying pies,
They sit and watch as one just flies.
Pastry tales may be far-fetched,
But sugar-coated hopes are etched.

The mailman dances with his cart,
Delivering dreams, playing the part.
With every bounce and every twirl,
He lights up the day, this cheerful squirrel.

At dusk, the stars begin to sigh,
While squirrels debate who'll touch the sky.
In these moments, all seems fine,
With laughter, grit, and a touch of wine.

Footprints on the Canvas of Time

An artist spills paint, oh what a scene,
Splashing colors on their jeans.
A masterpiece? Or a skyfall?
They couldn't tell, just having a ball.

Children giggle, ice cream in hand,
Building castles made of sand.
Each tower's wobble brings a cheer,
As seagulls plot and draw near.

A dog conducts the morning train,
Chasing sticks down memory lane.
With every bark, the world takes flight,
As dreams roll in like stars at night.

The mailboxes hold bloopers galore,
With love letters that slip and pour.
Each mishap spins a tale or two,
In quirky lines, life's funny view.

Breaths of the Unsung Chronicles

In whispers hushed, the garden sings,
Of garden gnomes and their wild flings.
With teacups balanced on their heads,
They dance the night while others dread.

A fish tells tales of ocean's spree,
Swapping stories 'neath the sea.
While crabs narrate their dire plight,
Of races lost, oh what a sight!

A raccoon who dreams of gold and fame,
Keeps raiding bins in hopes of claim.
With every feast, he hosts a show,
While humans watch, the stars aglow.

The cicadas chirp just for the laughs,
Creating symphonies from half-worn paths.
In these breaths, through every jest,
Life spins tales that we love best.

Journeys to the Inner Horizon

A snail sets out on a mighty quest,
To conquer hills—slow but blessed.
With every inch, the grass grows tall,
And daisies cheer, "He'll make it, y'all!"

A chicken dons a cape so bright,
Planning rescues deep in the night.
Feathers ruffle, wings all a-flap,
Her egg-ventures? An epic map!

The postman's hat floats like a dream,
Worn backwards, lost in thought's great scheme.
With every stop, he spins a yarn,
As dogs and cats join in the charm.

At twilight, frogs begin to croon,
Singing songs to the rise of the moon.
In laughter and joy, they leap and hop,
Reveling in moments that never stop.

Glimpses of the Invisible

In the fridge, a hidden snack,
A cheeky ghost plays peek-a-boo,
Dancing shadows on the wall,
Who knew silence loved a crew?

Underneath the bed, a sock,
Whispers of a missing mate,
Tickling toes in a soft mock,
Who knew lost socks went on dates?

The cat debates a sunny spot,
While shadows stretch like tales untold,
In this chaos, laughter's caught,
Life's absurd in joys we hold.

In every corner, secrets blend,
A wink from chairs and floors alike,
With every giggle, we transcend,
Invisible tales take flight and hike.

Parables from the Silence

With silent meals and laughing stew,
A comical chef juggles pies,
While forks gossip on the table,
Who knew utensils had such ties?

The dog looks wise, a sage in fur,
As whispers roam the backyard's green,
Every bark's a clever slur,
Mischief hides in the spaces unseen.

In the stillness of the night,
A tick-tock tales of clocks unfold,
Seconds giggle in their flight,
In the dark, mysteries bold.

The moon sneezes, the stars reply,
With twinkling giggles from afar,
Laughter flows in the midnight sky,
As silence sings, we are the stars.

Chronicles in the Stars

Once a comet lost its way,
Only to trip on a cosmic vine,
Chasing a wish that burned its day,
Forgot the map, but found the shine.

Constellations crack jokes in light,
As twinkling laughter fills the night,
Each planet rolls with comic grace,
In this vast and endless space.

A meteorite wearing a hat,
Claims to have dined with a galaxy,
The moon rolls eyes, says 'Stop that!'
Who knew rocks could be so ratty?

Tonight, the stars conspire in jest,
As each twinkle tells a riddle,
In every laughter, we find the rest,
Among the whoops, the world's a fiddle.

The Pathways We Create

Paved with laughter, roads are bright,
Each step echoes in a giggle,
A squirrel mocks with a sideways flight,
As grass blades tap dance and wiggle.

Sidewalks tell of trips and falls,
Mismatched shoes and sudden steer,
Every stumble, just life's calls,
Making footprints full of cheer.

Bicycles whiz with silly tunes,
While runners trip on cheerful beats,
Paths weave stories under moons,
In laughter's rhythm, life repeats.

Each twist and turn, a tale to share,
With friends who wink and prance and play,
In every moment, joy's laid bare,
Creating paths in a funny way.

Myriad Paths

We stumble down life's twisted ways,
Tripping over our own buffoonery.
With maps that lead to crazy days,
We laugh at our own pure lunacy.

Each choice a fork, a funny twist,
Navigating through zany dreams.
Missed turns that spark a chuckled fist,
As plans dissolve in comical schemes.

Unicycle rides and bubble baths,
All goals veer off into absurd.
Each mishap yields heartwarming laughs,
As we dodge life's well-placed absurd.

Yet through this chaos, we unite,
Finding joy in the wildest ride.
Random serenades, odd insights,
In this swirling tide, we abide.

One Heart

A beat that syncs with wobbling glee,
Like penguins on a frozen floor.
One heart, yet we dance so free,
Flapping arms and then we roar!

We share our pie and silly spins,
Claiming each little win or loss.
In mismatched socks, we now begin,
To celebrate each funny gloss.

Our hearts may dance in silly ways,
With tickles and snorts aplenty.
Through chaotic, joyful days,
Love's craziness feels so heavenly.

So here we are, two goofballs bright,
With laughter echoing through the night.

Underneath the Surface of Time

Underneath, time's a playful trick,
With clocks that laugh and tease us wrong.
Minutes stretch and then tick quick,
It's all a joyful, goofy song.

While seconds slip like soap in hands,
We dance like cats on rollerblades.
Life's rhythm makes unplanned bands,
Bursting forth in silly parades.

With calendars that mock our fate,
We scribble dates with crayon pens.
Time giggles hard — it's never straight,
As we try to make sense of trends.

Yet in this merry, topsy ride,
Laughter conquers every chime.

Synchronized Lives

Like dominoes, we wobble in line,
A synchronized dance, don't you see?
With misplaced steps, we intertwine,
Tripping on grace so blissfully.

In the world's greatest slapstick play,
We improvise roles, wild with flair.
Holding hands, we wade through the fray,
With wild outbursts and raucous air.

Mixed signals fly and giggles soar,
Every journey paved with quirks.
Together, we open each door,
Revising our fun through the lurks.

With hearts that beat a goofy throng,
We revel in moments and sing our song.

Entwined in Fate's Embrace

In life's great web, we weave and spin,
With tangled threads of joy and blunder.
Like kittens lost in paper bins,
We catapult into the thunder.

With every absurd twist and turn,
It's fate that thrives on sweet delight.
For every lesson yet to learn,
We chuckle through each raucous night.

So here we scream, we laugh, we play,
Through hiccups and mischief galore.
In every act, it's you I'll say,
Make life a dance forevermore.

Entwined, we paint our topsy tale,
Sharing laughter through every gale.

Fragments of Our Shared Journey

Once I danced with a frozen chicken,
Twirling under the moonlight, quite unwritten.
We laughed as it clucked and flapped around,
In the grocery aisle where joy was found.

Grandpa tried to teach me how to fish,
But he hooked his own hat - now that's a dish!
We cast not lines, but stories instead,
And the fish all giggled, happy and fed.

A car full of clowns, bright squeaky toys,
Our laughter echoed, mismatched plastic joys.
With cream pies in hand, we took a wild ride,
Chasing the sun, with friends all beside.

In p.j.s we raced, pajamas with flair,
Forgotten the contest, only giggles there.
A world of chaos, yet oh so divine,
These funny little moments forever entwined.

Inked Memories of Tomorrow

Once I tried to write with spaghetti, oh my,
Sauce on the page, how it flew, oh why?
Letters formed like noodles, wiggly and slick,
If only my book could read, it would kick!

We painted our futures with chocolate and cream,
Splatters of laughter, a sugary dream.
As we nibble on pages, oh what a sight,
These tasty tales, we shared day and night.

Then there was a cat, who stole my last pen,
He chewed through the ink like it was a gem.
Now poems are scribbled 'neath paws soft and wide,
A feline editor, with nothing to hide.

In the scribbles of life, joy rolled and twirled,
Every bite of mischief, a flavor unfurled.
These ink-stained adventures, so messy and bold,
Are the sweetest tales that for years we will hold.

Threads of a Thousand Lives

In a world of socks, mismatched they tread,
Each one has stories that need to be fed.
One sock said to another, 'I'm lost in the wash!'
A spinning adventure in a frothy frosh!

A turtle once wore a bright polka dot hat,
He claimed it was stylish, but it looked like a cat!
With each little stumble and tumble he took,
The world burst with laughter, it nearly shook.

Grandma's old quilt, a patchwork delight,
Hides secrets of feasts and jigs in the night.
Stitched with odd buttons and whispers of fun,
Each thread tells a tale, and the laughter won't run.

From silly-string battles to splatters of paint,
Threads of our past may seem far away, quaint.
But as we unwind, with a chuckle or two,
Life's yarn keeps rolling, it's all about you.

Beneath the Surface of Blue Skies

When clouds wear a hat, it's quite a silly sight,
Dancing and drifting, just out of pure flight.
Sunshine and rainbows throw a playful tease,
As we skip through puddles, taking life with ease.

A bumblebee tries to sing like a star,
With notes that buzz loud from near and far.
He fuels the flowers with laughter and cheer,
While we clap with joy, 'Let's dance, my dear!'

The squirrels throw parties deep in the trees,
With acorns as snacks and wildberries, please!
As we join in their music, a raucous affair,
Who knew nature's tune could spark laughter in air?

Under the vastness, where giggles collide,
We find all our dreams in the joy of the ride.
For life is a canvas, painted in glee,
Beneath the blue canopy, wild hearts run free.

Uncharted Territories of the Soul

In a world where socks go rogue,
And mismatched shoes steal the show,
We dance like no one's around,
While laughter echoes, heartbeats pound.

Every day's a new adventure,
Like a cat that thinks it's a squire,
Igniting dreams without a filter,
In a sitcom made of desire.

Juggling tasks like circus clowns,
Turning frowns into balloons,
Chasing whims on merry-go-rounds,
Who knew life could be such tunes?

So grab your hats and wigs today,
Let's paint the town in bright confetti,
With heart and soul, we find our way,
In a comedy so very zesty.

Sagas of Serendipity

In a café where spilled coffee reigns,
A muffin's dance begins to sway,
With croissants singing silly refrains,
Life's surprises brighten the day.

From lost keys found in oddest places,
To squirrels that steal your last french fry,
We bubble over with wild embraces,
As moments twist and fly up high.

Each stumble turns into a fortune,
As laughter spills from every seam,
Like mimes trapped inside a cartoon,
We jest through this absurdity dream.

So grab your giggles, don't delay,
With fortune's folly on our side,
Let's tumble through this funny play,
With a wink and a smile, we'll glide.

The Journey of Lost Voices

In a world where whispers chase their tails,
And echoes bounce like rubber balls,
We hum our songs with offbeat scales,
As fortune flirts and folly calls.

From flubbed lines in a morning toast,
To misheard quotes that tickle pink,
Each voice a riddle, a jolly ghost,
In life's funny, slippery sink.

We ponder thoughts that dance like mad,
On buses that take a wrong turn,
As laughter lights the thoughts we've had,
And lessons learned we always yearn.

So here's a toast to every blunder,
For in the chaos, joy ignites,
With every miss, we're pulling thunder,
And celebrate those quirky flights.

Epics of Everyday Life

With cereal wars in bowls of fate,
And toasters that pop with flair,
We sketch our lives on a paper plate,
While juggling whims in the morning air.

From socks that vanish, brave and bold,
To laundry piles that rise like towers,
As secret quests within unfold,
And mischief blooms at all the hours.

We write our tales on napkin scrolls,
With coffee stains that mark the plot,
In silly games, we find our roles,
In epic myths, we laugh a lot.

So join the dance of daily fun,
In every twist and silly strife,
As moments blend, the years outrun,
These are the joys that shape our life.

Marigold Memories in Autumn's Glow

Leaves crunching underfoot, oh what a sound,
Squirrels chasing tales that know no bounds.
Pumpkin spice whirls in the air so sweet,
As we laugh at our socks, mismatched on our feet.

Neighbors' cats plotting their grand heist,
Swiping our BBQ like a cat burglar's feast.
Marigolds blooming in colors so bright,
Remind us of summers that danced with delight.

Jokes poking fun at this aging crew,
Like our attempts at yoga, all quite askew.
Autumn hugs us in sweaters too tight,
As we share in the warmth of a campfire night.

Memories twirling like leaves in the breeze,
While we sip from mugs with stickers that tease.
Laughter echoes through crisp air we know,
In this fun, golden seasonal glow.

Echoing Laughter of Days Gone By

Remember the time that we lost the race?
You tripped on your shoelace, fell flat on your face.
We laughed so hard, we cried 'til we sighed,
While you insisted it was all just a ride.

Climbing tall trees, trying to touch the sky,
Splitting our sides as we dared each other to fly.
Sketchy stunts and wild dreams afloat,
Nothing compares to that one wobbly boat.

Fast-forward to now and it's pizza we crave,
Two-for-one specials, oh how we misbehave.
Replaying old tales as we stuff our pie,
With giggles that echo like stars way up high.

The days drift by, yet the laughter stays near,
Scraps of our stories, each joke crystal clear.
Life's like a sitcom that we all want to try,
With punchlines awakening the friend who won't die.

Silhouettes Against the Dusk

The sun dips low like a clumsy dancer,
Shadows stretched long, is it time for a prancer?
We twirl on the grass like we own the night,
One down, two to go, oh what a sight!

With watermelon smiles and laughter so loud,
We boast to the stars, feeling silly and proud.
Each twinkling light like an old fair tale,
Woven with friendship, no moment can fail.

There's a howling dog with his love-struck moan,
While we whisper secrets over ice cream bones.
The dusk wraps around us like soft buttered bread,
As we ponder the futures we dream in our heads.

Let's never forget, each misstep we make,
Like falling for pranks, or that giant cupcake.
Silhouettes spinning through twilight so bright,
In the dusk of our tales, laughter takes flight.

Tides of Unseen Waves

We wade in the surf, oh the splash and the giggle,
Each wave's a twist, a laugh, a wiggle.
At times we play sharks, with fins made of foam,
While seagulls critique our splash-down home.

Building sandcastles, but they never last,
A 'tsunami' knocks them away oh so fast!
We laugh till we choke, that's our sandy decree,
Life's tides are a dance – come wave along with me!

A hiccup of seagull, the beach hits a swoon,
With pop-up umbrellas and sunbaked prunes.
Each bite of our picnic is followed by yells,
As clouds tease our heads about those beachy spells.

Memories come crashing like the waves on the shore,
Laughing with friends, who could ask for more?
We ride on the tides of the joyous unknown,
In this ocean of fun, we are never alone.

www.ingramcontent.com/pod-product-compliance
Lightning Source LLC
Chambersburg PA
CBHW050307120526
44590CB00016B/2530